"I'm Going On a Diet Tomorrow"

(and Other Lies We Tell Ourselves)

How to

Effectively Resist

Temptation

"I'm Going On a Diet Tomorrow"

(and Other Lies We Tell Ourselves)

How to
Effectively Resist
Temptation

GREG LAURIE

 Dana Point, California

"I'm Going On a Diet Tomorrow"

Unless otherwise indicated, all Scripture quotations are taken from the New King James Version. Copyright © 1982 by Thomas Nelson, Inc. Used by permission. All rights reserved.

Scripture quotations marked (NLT) are taken from the *Holy Bible*, New Living Translation, copyright © 1986. Used by permission of Tyndale House Publishers, Inc., Wheaton, Illinois 60189. All rights reserved.

Scripture quotations marked (NIV) are taken from the Holy Bible, New International Version®. NIV®. Copyright © 1973, 1978, 1984 by International Bible Society. Used by permission of Zondervan Publishing House. All rights reserved.

ISBN 0-9762400-6-8

Printed in Canada.

Published by: Kerygma Publishing–Dana Point, California
Coordination: FM Management, Ltd.
Cover design: Christopher Laurie
Copyediting: Karla Pedrow
Interior Design: Highgate Cross+Cathey, Ltd.

Contents

God blesses the people who patiently
endure testing. Afterward they will
receive the crown of life that God
has promised to those who love him.
(James 1:12 NLT)

The **Problem** with *Diets*

Diet.
I hate the very word. I've actually tried them all. Sugar Busters? Been there, done that. Atkins? Bacon anyone? The Zone? Tried that one too. What's the new one? The South Beach Diet? Haven't tried that, but it looks like another meat-and-cheese regimen to me, with a palm tree thrown in for effect.

Don't get me wrong. I believe that diets work. Some work surprisingly well. But the problem is staying on them. The very word says it all: diet, as in "die." In other words, deny yourself. Abstain.

But consider the alternative. Your pants are fitting tighter. You find yourself tiring more easily. You take a shower and nothing below your waist gets wet. You get your shoes shined, and you have to take their word for it. The couch gets up when you do. Kids run to you to stay in the shade. You find yourself developing a dependence on the color black as a fashion staple. But there comes a point when even black cannot cover the reality. You have become a fat person. Or, you are well on your way to becoming one.

You might rationalize it by saying, "Well, there is just more of me to love now," but you know the truth. You really don't want to be overweight, so you actually start reading those e-mails about losing weight in ten days or less. Those before-and-after pictures suddenly capture your attention. Yet somehow, it all seems so unattainable.

THE BATTLE OF THE *Bulge*

It seems as the years have gone by, my pants size has gone up. For the longest time, I had a thirty-two-inch waist and weighed 155 pounds. Not bad for someone at five-eleven (and a half). Amazingly, this held despite many late-night meals and very bad choices. One of my favorites was at a taco joint I frequented. It was some wicked thing called a Macho Combo Burrito. I would pound down one of those just about every night at around ten o'clock. Today, that would not even be an option, not only because of the fact that I might be wearing it the next day, but also because my stomach would take revenge on me all night.

I became painfully aware that my metabolism was no longer what it used to be when I reached 188 pounds. I wasn't proud of it, but I couldn't deny what had been memorialized at Nordstrom, of all places. Parents had been invited to add their children's names and ages on tiles that would be permanently displayed on the floor of the children's department. So, a friend of mine thought it would be cute to put my name and weight on one of those tiles. There, next to "Amber, age 9" and "Nathan, age 6" is "Greg Laurie: 188." Either some people think I am older than I look, or they know the truth.

To make matters worse, after going on the Atkins diet, going off, and then back on again, I actually ballooned up to 200 pounds! My wife Cathe suggested that I was actually on a weight-gain diet. So, it was time for something new.

FOLLOWING IN THE FOOTSTEPS
OF *the Duchess of York*

I had some friends who have achieved some impressive results on the Weight Watchers program. Yet I cringed at the very thought. Weight Watchers? Doesn't that require going to meetings with strangers and weighing in? Don't they have "sharing" sessions in which they confess the struggles they face with weight gain? When I pressed one of these mysterious Weight Watchers named Paul about what you could or could not eat, he gave me vague answers, such as, "You can eat anything you want."

"Anything?"

"Yes, as long as you don't go over your points."

"Points? What are those?"

"Just go to one of the meetings," Paul urged.

It sounded like a cult to me. It appeared that I wouldn't know what it was really all about until I had been effectively brainwashed. But then I discovered that I could join Weight Watchers online. No meetings, no weigh-ins, and no sharing sessions. That suited me just fine. So, I started logging on to the Weight Watchers Web site and keeping a diary. There, I could type in foods I wasn't sure about and find out how many points they were. For instance, a taco was around six points, while a pizza was around thirteen. A hamburger was the same. With my allotment of twenty-seven points, I didn't want to squander them all before lunch. Exercise translated into extra credit, and therefore, the burger might become an option.

To remind me of why I was on this diet, I adopted the screen name, "Fat Boy."

UPWARD AND *Onward*

Since starting this book, I have gone back to Atkins and have returned again to Weight Watchers as well. How's that for fickle? A friend of mine says I must have the cleanest mind around, because I am always changing it. By the time you read this, I may have moved on to my own version of previous diets, such as the Atkins Buster or The South Beach Sugar Zone. Who knows?

The problem is, once I begin to make progress on any of these weight loss regimens, I start to sabotage it. I am a diet backslider. I tend to fall off the diet wagon, so to speak. In my attempt to lose weight, I will take two steps forward and three back. "Oh look, I lost three pounds!" I will say. "I think I'll celebrate with a pizza!" Therefore, I tend to be starting a new diet, or breaking the rules of the one I am supposedly on.

Awhile back, my wife Cathe and I were out with another couple for dinner. After dining on some delicious grilled fish and vegetables, I was presented with the offer of dessert. Even the way the servers approach the subject gives you an indication of where it will lead.

"Can I tempt you with a dessert?"

"Tempt?"

"But it's not a sin to be tempted, right?"

So I listen. They use verbiage that should tip us off, such as "sinfully delicious." Then there is the "wicked devil's food cake." It just so happens that this particular restaurant has my favorite dessert of all time. It's some savory little dish called Flan Cake. My wife could explain how they do it, but it's basically a moist cake in custard sauce with freshly whipped cream and strawberries. Then, to finish it off, caramel sauce is drizzled artfully over the top of it all. So, it was easy for me to say "no thank you" as the server went through the dessert options—until she came to Flan Cake, that is. Like a shark instinctively responding to the smell of blood, I was already imagining the Flan Cake in front of me.

So, I confidently declared, "Yeah, let's order that, because I'm going on a diet tomorrow!" Everyone at the table started laughing. When I asked why, they reminded me that I said this every time this particular dessert was offered. It dawned on me that I had been rationalizing my Flan Cake indulgence for a long time. I told them, jokingly, "That would be a good title for a book: *I'm Going on a Diet Tomorrow … and Other Lies We Tell Ourselves.*"

So, here you hold in your hands the result of that endeavor.

Excusable *Behavior* 2

Please understand, this is not a book about diets for the most part (probably because I haven't completely figured that out yet). Rather, this is a book about rationalizations that get us into trouble, how we talk ourselves into bad behavior, and why we don't do the right thing when we know we should. It's a book about how to stop making excuses and start effectively resisting temptation.

We all know what it's like to justify something we are about to do with a clever excuse. You know the routine:

"I know this is wrong, but everybody's doing it."

"I'll know when to stop."

"I'll quit tomorrow."

"It's not my fault."

"I can't help it—I'm under so much stress."

"I'm not hurting anyone but myself."

"I deserve this."

"I'm not that bad."

"It's totally acceptable in other cultures."

"God understands my unique needs."

Do any of these sound familiar? As someone once said, "An excuse is nothing more than the skin of a reason stuffed with a lie." In other words, an excuse is a downright lie. We usually offer them when we don't want to do something that we know we really ought to do. Is there anyone who actually looks forward to mowing a lawn or taking out the trash or putting gas in the car? I don't know why, but I will put off filling up my car as long as possible. Maybe it's because I think I will somehow save money by waiting. I finally break down when that little light (sometimes called an "idiot light," for good reason) comes on. I will reluctantly pull into the nearest gas station and do that which I dreaded, which is, frankly, not that bad after all.

I do this with cleaning and straightening up too. For instance, I will allow my office to get pretty messy before I break down and put things in their proper place. Books are stacked on books, papers are piled on papers, and the morning latte, half-drunk, rests on the last available flat surface. Like a whirlwind, I will sweep through and bring things back to a place of order. But I will put this off as long as possible. I am the classic procrastinator, operating by the adage, "Don't do today what you can put off until tomorrow."

But I'm not the only excuse-maker out there. I would bet that you are one too. Otherwise, why would you have picked up this book? Take heart. There are plenty more of us out there across our great country. An article in *USA Today* dealt with this penchant we have for making excuses.

It pointed out that each of us fibs at least fifty times per day. According the article, "we lie about our age, our income, or our accomplishments … and we use lies to escape embarrassment." The most commonly used excuses are:

"I wasn't feeling well."

"I didn't want to hurt your feelings."

"I was only trying to help."

"I was just kidding."

And that all-time classic, "The check is in the mail."[1]

LAME *Excuses*

I found a Web site that lists actual excuses people have used to get out of showing up for work. Apparently their employers thought these were such whoppers that they should be shared with others as a form of entertainment. Here are a few of them:

"I won't be in today. My fish is sick and I need to take it to the vet."

"I won't be in today because I have come down with Spring fever."

"I can't come to work today because the city is paving my street and I can't get out!"

"I will not be in to work today because my parents' dog died."

Left on an employer's answering machine: "Sorry boss, I won't be in for three days. Went to see my sister off on her cruise to the Bahamas ... darn ship left with me still on it. The captain refuses to turn back."

At least one guy who called in was honest about it. He said to his boss, "I am sick with the lack—the lack of ambition."[2]

Then there are those doozies people will tell to law enforcement when they have been pulled over. One obviously inebriated man was pulled over by the California Highway Patrol because he was driving the wrong way on an Interstate highway. The officer who pulled him over shouted, "Sir, do you know you are driving down the Interstate the wrong way?"

The drunk responded, "How do you know? You don't know where I live!" Ah, the logic of an alcohol-soaked brain. Needless to say, this man spent the night in jail.

Another man pulled over for speeding actually said to the officer, "Please excuse me from this speeding ticket. You see, my wife ran off with a state policeman and when I saw your flashing lights, I didn't stop, because I thought you might be the trooper who was trying to bring her back to me!" I don't know if he was given a ticket for speeding or not, but he should have been arrested for giving a lame excuse. As George Washington said, "It is better to offer no excuse than a bad one."

The fact is, we have all heard, and even used, excuses at one time or another, and most of the time, they are not all that creative. Since humanity's beginning in the Garden, we have made them.

THE FIRST *Excuse*

The first recorded excuse was made by the first man himself, Adam. Talk about a guy who had it made in the shade. He was created by God and placed in a pure paradise that would make Maui look like a parking lot. Adam was surrounded by intense, unimaginable beauty and splendor. There was no pollution, no discomfort, and best of all, no death. Adam's basic job description was to enjoy, watch over, and discover all that God had made. Best of all, the Lord himself would show up each and every day, and He and Adam would talk over the events of the day. It would happen just as the sun was setting, before nightfall.

So there was Adam, living large and enjoying fellowship with God himself. Each day, he would be greeted by a new discovery of what his Friend and Creator had made. But something was missing in Adam's life. Sure, he liked to hang out with animals, admire the scenery, and visit with his Creator every day, but he wanted someone to share all this with. But that someone did not yet exist.

One day, the Lord had Adam fall into a very deep sleep. When he awoke, there, for the first time, was that someone he had been searching for. He called her Eve. She was beautiful to behold, and she became Adam's closest friend, second only to God himself. You could not ask for a better life.

But God had given a dangerous ability to Adam and his new bride. They could choose to do right—and even wrong. "But why?" we ask. "Why didn't God just make Adam want to do the right thing and not give him the ability to choose?" It's because God wanted voluntary love, not forced affection. Would you want someone to be your friend because they had to or because they wanted to? God is no different in that regard.

THE CHOICE

So God gave to His two finest creations the ability to choose, and you probably know what they did. They ate of the forbidden fruit. Now, it's often stated that this forbidden fruit was an apple. I don't know where that came from. The Bible makes no mention of an apple, but only fruit. Considering the fact they lived in a perfect paradise, there had to be something very attractive about this forbidden fruit that caught their eye. Who knows? Maybe it even pulsated. According to the Book of Genesis, we know that it was attractive to the eye. Enough said; it just flat out looked good. Really good. It probably smelled pretty great too.

So, despite the fact that their best friend God told them to not do it, they took a small bite. They might have said, "It's really all right, because we won't ever do it again!" But they wouldn't have to, because one time would be enough. More than enough. We are still living with the ramifications of that little taste test to this very day: aging, disease, death, and worst of all, separation from God himself. It all came from the sin that began in a paradise.

GOD ALWAYS KEEPS HIS *Appointments*

That day, the Lord showed up for his usual appointment with Adam. But for the first time, Adam was nowhere to be found. Genesis tells us, "And they heard the sound of the Lord God walking in the garden in the cool of the day … " (Gen 3:8).

So God called out, "Adam, where are you?" Needless to say, God didn't say this because He was ignorant of the whereabouts of His child, any more than a father playing hide-and-seek with his two-year-old is unaware of his exact hiding place. God was looking for his friend to come clean and to admit what he had done.

Having the Lord himself show up for a chat was normally the high point of Adam's day. We are told that God came in the "cool of the day"—what a beautiful picture that brings to mind. The day was ending, night had not yet fallen, the sun was setting, and the air was cool. The already beautiful Eden was bathed in a warm, golden light. Adam must have looked forward to it each and every day. I know that I would have. When something would come up, Adam might have thought, "I must talk to the Lord about that in our time together late this afternoon." Or perhaps there was a new discovery in this Garden he was commanded to tend that he could personally ask God about: "Lord, how did You ever come up with this design?"

It is interesting to note that God did not come in "the heat of the day," say twelve o'clock noon, so Adam would think God was coming in the heat of passion. He didn't come in the early morning, lest Adam think that God couldn't wait to nail him for his sin. After all, the Bible teaches, "The Lord is merciful and gracious, slow to anger, and abounding in mercy" (Ps. 103:8). Instead, the Lord came in the cool of the day, loving, patient, hurt yet understanding, but at the same time, demanding confession.

Now, instead of looking forward with joy to this daily event as he usually did, Adam shrank from it. That which was once desired was now dreaded because of sin. Sin will do that to you. It will quench your appetite for what you really need and increase your appetite for what can ultimately destroy you. Adam had plenty of time to think about what he had done. What once had been so exciting and intoxicating was now having its ultimate way. That dead, empty feeling was sinking in.

Sin had done, and was doing, its wicked work in the first couple. Adam was experiencing something he had never known before: guilt. It was gnawing at him, giving him no rest. "If only I hadn't taken that bite," he thought. He sat there alone with his own tormenting thoughts when suddenly a familiar voice was heard.

"Adam?"

"It's the Lord!" Adam thought. "What am I going to say? How can I possibly explain this?" So Adam grabbed Eve and they quickly ducked for cover.

The Lord spoke again, "Adam, where are you?"

Notice that instead of man calling out to God, it was God calling out to man. And that, by the way, is one very significant thing that distinguishes the Christian faith from any other belief system or religion in the world today. In all religions apart from Christianity, for all practical purposes, man is calling out to God. But the Bible presents God calling out to man. Just as He called out to Adam in the Garden long ago, He calls out to you today. But why did God call out to His wayward son? Among other things, it was meant to convince of sin. That is because we often rationalize our sin in such a way that we don't even think we have done something wrong.

What tone of voice do you think God used? Do you think it was harsh and loud, as in, "Adam, where are you, you miserable failure?" I don't think so. Perhaps the Lord called out in bewilderment and confusion: "Adam, where are you? I can't find you!" Again, I don't think so. I think it was the voice of a hurt but still loving Father.

So here was Adam, hiding behind his "cover-up." Satan had promised that if Adam and Eve ate of the forbidden fruit, they would be "like God, knowing good and evil" (Gen. 3:5). So God was essentially saying, "Well, Adam, is that how it is? Or did the devil lie to you?" The same thing happens to us. Satan whispers in our ear, "Go for it! This will be fun! No one will ever know!"

The Lord was saying, "Is that how it turned out? Are you pleased with the outcome?"

"Where are you?" really is a fascinating question for the

Creator to ask. God, of course, knew exactly where Adam and Eve were. He was not calling them to get information, but rather a confession. He wanted them to confront what they had done so they could set it right and be restored to fellowship with himself.

Jesus told the story of a boy who ran away from home. We know him as the prodigal son. But before that young man returned to the comfort and security of home, he had to see his real condition. Jesus said that "he came to himself" (Luke 15:17), which simply means that he came to his senses. In the same way, God wanted Adam to come out of the stupor of sin and admit his real condition. But why? Was it to rub Adam's face in it, so to speak? Hardly. The reason God said this is the same reason His Holy Spirit will convict us, even using guilt. It is to awaken us. That is so we won't run away from God, but to Him. But Adam was not ready for that yet.

Maybe God is saying much the same to you right now:

"I missed you in church this last week!" *Where are you?*

"I missed hearing from you in prayer today!" *Where are you?*

"You read your Bible this morning, but with such an absent mind." *Where are you?*

Where are you spiritually in your life right now? Are you in the place you need to be? Are you satisfied with your spiritual condition, or does a change need to take place? Before you can find your way to what you need, you must first recognize where you are.

Let's say you wanted to come to our church for a Sunday morning service, so you give us a call. When I pick up the phone, you ask, "How do we get to Harvest Christian Fellowship? We want to worship with you this morning!"

You know, of course, what my next question will be: "Where are you?" Now, why would I ask that of you? Is it because I'm really nosy and want to know your every step? Hardly. The reason I'm asking where you are is so that I can tell you how to get where you want to go.

So, why did God ask Adam, "Where are you?" It was so He could tell him how to get back to paradise.

Perhaps you're thinking, "I don't know where I am. I only know that I am not where I ought to be, nor where I want to be. That's all I can say." But that is good. It's a beginning.

Finally Adam answered, "I heard Your voice in the garden, and I was afraid because I was naked; and I hid myself" (Gen. 3:10).

God immediately responded, "Who told you that you were naked?" (v. 11). Now, why did God ask such a question? Didn't He already know the answer to this one as well? Yes, but He wanted Adam to know too.

Have you ever known that your child did something wrong and you confronted him? You might have asked him, "Did you do such and such? Why did you do that? Do you think this is all right for you to do?" Did you ask your child these questions because you personally didn't know what was right or wrong? Of course not. You asked these questions because you wanted to make sure your child knew it was wrong. You were looking for an admission of wrongdoing, a confession of sin. And that's exactly what God was looking for too. God wanted nothing short of a full-blown confession.

Adam then offered up the first recorded excuse ever given by man. In many ways, it's the mother of all whoppers in the excuse category, because it failed to acknowledge personal responsibility and then conveniently placed the blame on another. So instead of acknowledging his sin, Adam offered this excuse: "The woman whom You gave to be with me, she gave me of the tree, and I ate" (v. 12). This shows the absolute wickedness of sin. Eve was deceived. The Scripture is clear on this. But Adam, to his discredit, willfully and knowingly sinned. If that wasn't bad enough, he had the audacity to actually blame God for it. He was saying, in essence, "You, Lord, have sinned! This is your doing, Lord. It's the woman You gave me! You're the one who brought Eve along!"

THE CURSE AND ITS *Cure*

How easily God could have struck down Adam where He stood. Like a spoiled little child, Adam dared to suggest that it was God, and not him, who had failed. God had literally put Adam in paradise with every possible comfort, surrounded by such breathtaking beauty that has never been seen since. Yet in spite of all this, Adam lashed out at the very God who gave all this to him. But as Lamentations 3:22 reminds us, "The unfailing love of the Lord never ends! By his mercies we have been kept from complete destruction" (NLT).

But neither Adam nor Eve convinced God with their excuses. God busted His wayward children, and separation from Him resulted.

How did all of this happen in the first place? Temptation was entertained—and then given in to.

Temptation
Can Do
Us Some *Good*

We generally think that all temptation is bad. Yet it may surprise you to know that testing, and even temptation, can have a positive effect. The Bible tells us, "Blessed is the man who endures temptation; for when he has been approved, he will receive the crown of life which the Lord has promised to those who love Him" (James 1:12).

Right off the bat, we learn three things about temptation from this verse:

1. It can be endured: "Blessed is the man [or woman] who endures temptation. ... "
2. There is a reward for the person who endures it: "He [or she] will receive the crown of life. ..."
3. You will be a happy person if you resist temptation's pull: "Blessed is the man [or woman]. ..."

Martin Luther once said, "One Christian who has been tempted is worth a thousand who haven't." It also has been said, "Christians are a lot like tea bags. You don't know what they are made of until you put them in hot water."

You never know when temptation will come your way. I heard about a young salesman who went to bid on a job for his firm. He couldn't help but notice a competitor's bid on the purchasing agent's desk. Unfortunately, the actual figure was covered by a can of juice. But the temptation to see the amount became too much, and the salesman lifted the can. His heart sank as he watched thousands of BBs pour from the bottomless container and scatter across the floor. He got busted for giving in to his temptation. And you will too.

That is why we must learn to resist it. Benjamin Franklin once wrote, "It is easier to suppress the first desire than to satisfy all that follow it."

WHAT YOU NEED TO KNOW *About Temptation*

We are about to look at the following aspects of temptation:

1. When does it come?
2. Where does it come from?
3. Whom does it come to?
4. Where is the best place to be when it comes?
5. What is the primary weapon we should use to resist it?

In Luke 4, we find the story of Jesus being tempted by Satan. I would like to consider this story and see what truths we can pull out of it to help us in the daily barrage of temptations that come our way at breakneck speed. Jesus set the example. Now let's set the scene.

Jesus was now ready to officially begin His public ministry. But before that could happen, He had to take a couple of very important steps. The first was to be baptized. The other was to face his temptation in the wilderness. But why?

Jesus was not sinful; therefore, He did not need to undergo the "baptism of repentance" that his cousin, John the Baptizer, was advocating. The reason Jesus did this was to set an example for all of us. And that, by the way, is why He faced this series of temptations as well.

It is essential we see that Jesus faced Satan as a man. In other words, He did not use His divine power to be delivered or to run Satan out. He showed us what to do and how to do it when one is tempted. He occupied ground that we, too, can occupy as we heed the words of Philippians 2:5: "Let this mind be in you which was also in Christ Jesus. … " This brings us to the first question I raised.

WHEN DOES TEMPTATION *Come?*

Answer: Often after great times of blessing. It was after this time of great blessing in the life of our Lord that it hit: "Then Jesus, being filled with the Holy Spirit, returned from the Jordan and was led by the Spirit into the wilderness, being tempted for forty days by the devil … " (Luke 4:1–2).

Again, Jesus had just been baptized. The Holy Spirit had come upon Him in the form of a dove, and the Father spoke from heaven. Then Satan bared his teeth. Then temptation came. After the dove came the devil. After the blessing came the time of testing. The two often go hand-in-hand.

So, you might be in church some Sunday, being blessed and encouraged in your faith, and right after the service—perhaps even during—that impure thought, that ungodly impulse tugs on you. Understand, that is to be expected. History tells us that when Hitler invaded the European nations during the early years of World War II, in almost every situation, he attacked on a weekend. You see, Hitler knew the various parliaments would not be in session, which would make it more difficult to react swiftly to an invasion.

How like the enemy of our souls, the devil, who is always watching and waiting for an opportune time to attack. He is waiting for that moment when we are the most vulnerable. It just may be at a time when we think we are the strongest, as 1 Corinthians 10:12 warns us: "Therefore let him who thinks he stands take heed lest he fall."

WHERE DOES TEMPTATION *Come From?*

It is vital that we know we play a key role in our own temptation:

> Let no one say when he is tempted, "I am tempted by God"; for God cannot be tempted by evil, nor does

He Himself tempt anyone. But each one is tempted
when he is drawn away by his own desires and enticed.
Then, when desire has conceived, it gives birth to sin;
and sin, when it is full-grown, brings forth death. Do
not be deceived, my beloved brethren.
(James 1:13–16)

Satan needs our cooperation to give in to his temptation. Where there is no desire on our part, there is no
temptation to speak of. Think about it. You have never
seen an insurance salesman at the cemetery, trying to
make a sale. That's because you can't sell something to
someone who isn't listening or caring. The same is true of
us. The devil needs our cooperation.

Here is something every believer needs to understand.
We have three enemies we contend with as Christians:
the world, the flesh, and the devil.

The flesh, with its evil desires, is the internal foe.

The world, with its enticements, is the external foe.

Satan, with his temptations, is the infernal foe.

But when you get down to it, we have ourselves to
thank, for the most part, when we give in to temptation.
Jesus said, "What comes out of a man, that defiles a man"
(Mark 2:21). Paul echoed this thought when he wrote,
"Do you not know that to whom you present yourselves
slaves to obey, you are that one's slaves whom you obey,
whether of sin leading to death, or of obedience leading
to righteousness?" (Rom. 6:16). Yes, it's our own sinful
nature that is to blame for most of our problems.

THE SCORPION AND *the Tortoise*

This reminds me of the fable of the scorpion and the tortoise. As you may know, scorpions can't really swim. So one day, a scorpion that wanted to cross a pond found a rather unsuspecting tortoise and asked if he would give him a lift to the other side. The tortoise exclaimed, "Are you joking? You'll sting me while I'm swimming and I'll drown."

"My dear tortoise," laughed the scorpion, "if I were to sting you, you would drown, and I'd go down with you. Now, where is the logic in that?"

"You've got a point there," reasoned the tortoise. "Hop on." The scorpion climbed aboard, and halfway across the pond, he carefully aimed his powerful stinger and gave the tortoise everything he had.

As they both were sinking to the bottom, the tortoise, resigned to his fate, turned to the scorpion and said, "Do you mind if I ask you something? You said there is no logic in your stinging me. Why did you do it?"

"It has nothing to do with logic," the drowning scorpion replied. "It's just my nature!"

In a way, that is a very accurate way of defining temptation and why we are so weak. In the immortal words of the scorpion, "It's just our nature."

We all have a natural, inward bent to do the wrong thing. We like to think that our bad behavior is a direct result of our upbringing, environment, and so on. Although these things do indeed have an influence on us, the primary reason we think and do the wrong thing is because of our sinful nature.

"I COULDN'T RESIST *Myself.*"

When my son Jonathan was still very young, I sent him to bed one night and told him, "Now turn off the light. No more video games, OK?"

He agreed. But a bit later, I noticed a familiar, blue glow coming from beneath the door, which I opened and caught little Jonathan red-handed, blasting away at enemy ships via video imagery.

When I demanded an explanation, he blurted out, "Dad, I didn't mean to, but I couldn't resist myself." It was so cute that I just let it go (and unplugged the video game).

But he was really on to something. We love to blame the devil and others for our spiritual stumbles and falls. But the truth is, it's just our nature. Or, as that young theologian, Jonathan Laurie, said, "I couldn't resist myself." When we get tempted and give in, we like to conveniently place the blame on someone or something else.

Sometimes we even want to blame God for our missteps. We will lamely say something along the lines of, "God just gave me more than I could handle!" Talk about passing the buck! Again, this is what Adam essentially did in the Garden, and it's what we do when we can't own up to our own complicity in our sinful choices.

The Bible clearly refutes this kind of thinking in reminding us, "Let no one say when he is tempted, 'I am tempted by God'; for God cannot be tempted by evil, nor does He Himself tempt anyone" (James 1:13).

Scripture also tells us that God will never give us more then we can handle:

> No temptation has seized you except what is common to man. And God is faithful; he will not let you be tempted beyond what you can bear. But when you are tempted, he will also provide a way out so that you can stand up under it. (1 Cor. 10:13 NIV)

WHOM DOES TEMPTATION *Come to?*

In a broad sense, everyone is tempted. At the same time, without question, the enemy focuses his attacks on those who are young in the faith and those who are making a difference for the kingdom of God.

I think practically every new Christian doubts their salvation in some way, shape, or form. It might be the day after you asked Jesus to come into your life, and the devil whispers in your ear, "Do you actually believe that God would forgive someone like you? Do you really think your sins are forgiven and Jesus lives in your heart? Get real! You psyched yourself into it!" We may not feel God at that particular moment, and as a result, start believing this is the truth. But please know that this is common, and even to be expected to a large degree, among those who are very new in the faith.

In the Parable of the Sower, Jesus gave us some insight into how Satan works. He compared God's Word to seed being sown by a farmer, but some of it falls on the road, and the ever-watching birds swoop down quickly and scoop it up. Jesus then went on to interpret these words: "And these are the ones by the wayside where the word is sown. When they hear, *Satan comes immediately* and takes away the word that was sown in their hearts" (Mark 4:15, emphasis mine).

Note the words, "Satan comes immediately." This strategy of getting someone to doubt his or her faith goes all the way back to the Garden of Eden. We have already looked at this story together, but again, remember how God had placed Adam and Eve in the paradise called Eden and specifically told them to keep their distance from the Tree of Knowledge of Good and Evil. Yet we find Eve foolishly hanging around that very tree and setting herself up. I guess she "couldn't resist herself." Satan came and said to her, "Did God really say you must not eat any of the fruit in the garden?" (Gen. 3:1 NLT). The devil was saying, "Did God really say what you thought He said?"

A PRETTY GIRL *Comes Calling*

I remember experiencing this major temptation in my life right after my conversion. I was in high school and just days old in the faith, excited about what God had done for me. I even wore a little button on my shirt with a drawing of Jesus on it.

I went to one of my classes and noticed a very attractive girl looking at me and smiling. Now, I had noticed this girl before, but frankly, she had never noticed me. Suddenly, seemingly out of nowhere, she was making eyes at me! The Christians I knew told me that I would be tempted after my conversion, and I wondered if this would be it. I didn't have to wait long to find out, because just as class let out, this cute little dish sashayed up to me and said, "Hi. What's your name?"

I forgot my name momentarily, stunned by her sudden interest in me.

"You are really cute, Greg," she cooed. "I've never noticed you before."

I was dumbfounded.

Then she looked into my eyes and said, "I would really like to get to know you better. Hey, my parents have this house up in the mountains, and they will be gone this weekend. Want to go up with me?"

I knew this had to be a temptation, because things like this just didn't happen to me. I wondered, "Why is this happening to me now when I can't act on it? Talk about bad timing!" Then it dawned on me. This wasn't bad timing. It was precise timing—from hell. Satan was hitting me where I was weak and when I was young in the faith.

I got excited, not so much about the temptation, but

about the opportunity to resist. I remember thinking to myself, "If Satan wants to trip me up this much, God must have something really special in store for me." So, by the grace of God, I said no to her. She walked off in a huff, and I'm sure she quickly found another taker for her little mountain getaway.

I felt a great sense of relief and joy after I made, as a new follower of Jesus Christ, my first conscious decision to turn away from what I wanted to do. And I was blessed, or happy, as the Scripture says we will be when we resist temptation (see James 1:12).

This is why Satan attacked Jesus. He was a threat. And this is why he will attack you, because you, as His follower, are a threat too. As the great British preacher C. H. Spurgeon once wrote, "You don't kick a dead horse."

You might protest and say, "But Greg, I never get tempted to do the wrong thing!" If that is the case, then you must be either dead or worthless, because if you are really following Jesus, then you will be tempted. It's not a matter of if—just when and how.

TEMPTATION KNOCKS AT *Every Door*

Why did Satan tempt Samson, David, Joseph, and Peter? It was because of the damage they were all doing to his kingdom. So be forewarned. When you pray, "Use me, Lord. Let my life make a difference," then you'd better brace yourself. The enemy won't sit idly by.

I'm not saying that Satan doesn't play a part when you

fall into temptation or that his power is not considerable (though not as considerable as you might think). Although Satan plays a part in our temptation, we are ultimately responsible for our own spiritual success or failure. (For more helpful teaching on resisting temptation, I would refer you to my book, *The Great Compromise*.)

God knows how much we can take. When He lets His children go through fiery trials, He always keeps one eye on them and one finger on the thermostat. Remember, He has made a way of escape in the midst of every temptation. Therefore, if we succumb to the enticements and temptations of the devil, we must take responsibility for that.

THE BLAME *Game*

I've already mentioned that Adam blamed Eve. While Adam was responsible for his own fall, Eve was responsible for hers too. "Isn't it true that Eve was deceived by the Serpent to eat the forbidden fruit?" you might ask. True. She was. But the Serpent wouldn't have had the opportunity to deceive her if she wasn't listening. That is why the Bible says, "Resist the devil and he will flee from you" (James 4:7). If Eve had resisted the devil, he could not have influenced her as he did. Certainly, the devil tempted her, but she was in the wrong place at the wrong time, listening to the wrong voice. As a result, she did the wrong thing.

THE CROCODILE *Hunter*

You may remember some time ago when the over-excited Steve Irwin of *The Crocodile Hunter* fame, with his infant close at hand, fed a rather large croc a piece of meat. There was a great public outcry as people wondered why he would take such a needless chance. Irwin's response was that he wanted to get his child croc savvy. The problem with that was, one stumble, and Steve's baby could have been a croc snack. When asked about the danger of this, he said, "It's all about perceived danger; I was in complete control."

What if he had fallen? "For that to take place," said Irwin, "a meteorite would have had to come out of the sky and hit Australia."[3]

But my question is, why take a risk like that? Why push it? In the same way, never, ever lower your guard or think you are somehow immune or temptation-proof. It is often when we feel the strongest that we are actually the most vulnerable. Just when we feel the most secure within ourselves, just when we think our spiritual life is at its strongest, just when we're convinced that our doctrine is the soundest, our morals are the purest, and our lives are the most stable, it is then we should be the most dependent on the Lord. We should be vigilant to stand guard during these times of apparent safety, more than at any other time. When we think we've reached some spiritual plateau, this is when we are in the most jeopardy.

STRONG MEN WITH *Big Weaknesses*

Sometimes the weakest Christian is not in as much danger as the strongest one. You see, our strongest virtues can also be our greatest vulnerabilities. Consider some of the great personalities of the Bible. They experienced times of vulnerability too. Take the following, very human examples of this.

The great lawgiver, Moses, was known as the meekest man on the face of the earth, yet pride and presumption dealt him a fatal blow.

Samson, the great Judge of Israel and a man of supernatural strength, fell because he yielded to his natural desires.

Simon Peter discovered that in the area where he believed himself to be the strongest, he was actually weak.

The miracle-working prophet of lore, Elijah, who was distinguished by great bravery and boldness, was paralyzed by fear.

So you see, we must never rest on our laurels. There are always new mountains to climb, new obstacles to overcome, and yes, more temptations to resist. The mature believer realizes there is always a long way to go. He or she realizes there is always the potential and propensity for sin within.

JUST A LITTLE BIT WON'T HURT ... *Will It?*

"Oh, I can handle a little marijuana. It won't be a problem."
"One drink won't hurt!"

"Just a little porn can't be all that bad. I won't do it again."

"A little flirting is fun. What harm could it bring?

Famous last words. And speaking of those, have you ever heard the last words of Bucky O'Neill? He was an Arizona lawyer, miner, cowboy, gambler, newspaperman, sheriff, and congressman. He was also one of the most important members of Teddy Roosevelt's Rough Riders during the Spanish-American War. Moments prior to the famous charge up Kettle Hill, O'Neill was standing up, smoking a cigarette, and joking with his troops while under withering fire from the ridge. One of his sergeants shouted to him above the noise, "Captain, a bullet is sure to hit you!"

To which O'Neill shouted back his reply, "Sergeant, the Spanish bullet isn't made that will kill me." No sooner had O'Neill uttered those words than he was hit and killed by a bullet.

No one is bulletproof or temptation-proof.

KEEP *Moving!*

Never lower your guard. Always go forward spiritually. I once heard the story of a young captain who served in the ranks of Napoleon's army. When he was recommended for a military promotion, Napoleon asked why this particular man had been suggested.

His commanding officer answered, "Well, out on the battlefield several days ago, he displayed unusual courage and, as a result, a victory was won."

"Good," Napoleon replied. "What did he do the *next day?*"

We may talk about what we did for the Lord ten years ago or ten weeks ago. But what did you do the next day? What about today?

Are you preparing for tomorrow? We can't live in the past. Our relationship with Christ should be fluid and growing. It requires constant maintenance and cultivation. As the Bible exhorts us,

> But you, dear friends, must continue to build your lives on the foundation of your holy faith. And continue to pray as the Holy Spirit directs you. Live in such a way that God's love can bless you as you wait for the eternal life that our Lord Jesus Christ in his mercy is going to give you. (Jude 1:20–21 NLT)

The day we stop being built up on the foundation of our faith is the day our faith will begin the process of breaking down. Scripture reminds us that God's mercies are new every morning (see Lam. 3:23) and that we must take up our cross daily and follow Him (see Luke 9:23).

We must always be moving forward spiritually. If we fail to this, we will become sitting ducks, more vulnerable than ever to the enticements and temptations of the devil. Though it has been said many times, it is still true: The best defense is a good offense. The best way not to go backward is to keep going forward.

So let's not be satisfied with what we once did for Christ. Let's not live in the past. Let's press forward, taking up our crosses daily and following Him.

THE HUNTER AND *The Bear*

The devil knows that one of the most effective ways to pull someone down is through the deadly and very effective ploy of compromise. More have been brought down by this strategy of his than perhaps by any other. It reminds me of a story I heard once about a hunter and a bear. The hunter went deep into the woods in search of a bear. It seems he wanted to shoot one and skin it for its coat. After a long wait, the hunter finally had a huge brown bear in his sight. He wrapped his finger slowly around the trigger, and holding the barrel steady, he aimed for the center of the hulking animal's very large forehead. Just as he was preparing to squeeze the trigger, the bear turned around, and catching the hunter by surprise, said in a soft voice, "Wait! Let's talk this thing over! Isn't it better to talk than to shoot?"

The hunter was so surprised that he lowered his gun.

The bear thanked him and said, "Now, what is it that you want? Can't we negotiate?

The hunter replied, "Well, actually all I want is a fur coat!"

"Good," the bear said. "All I want is a meal!"

As the two sat down to negotiate, the hunter dropped his guard and laid his gun down on a big, gray rock. Then the two disappeared into the forest. After awhile, the bear came back out, alone. Apparently, the negotiations had been successful. The bear had a full stomach, and the hunter had his fur coat.

That's how compromise works.

WHERE IS THE BEST PLACE TO BE
When Temptation Comes?

The short answer is, in the will of God. Scripture tells us that Jesus "was led by the Spirit into the wilderness, being tempted for forty days by the devil" (Luke 4:1–2). He was in the will of God.

Far too often, we are out of the will of God, essentially bringing temptation on ourselves. What makes resisting temptation difficult for many people is that they don't want to discourage it completely. Many people want to be delivered from temptation, but would like to keep in touch. To pray against temptation and yet rush into places of vulnerability is like thrusting your fingers into a fire and praying they won't be burned.

PRONE TO *Wander*

You may remember some of the steps that led to the fall of Simon Peter. Sadly, he denied the Lord three times. That actual denial happened near the house of the High Priest of Israel, where Jesus was being examined on trumped-up charges. There, warming himself by the nearby fire from the chill of his soul, the denials began.

Peter was outside of the will of God, and he had already taken other steps to make himself even more vulnerable, like arguing with Jesus and not praying when the Lord told him to. He was just an accident waiting to happen. And it did.

When someone recognized Peter as one of the followers of Christ, his denial fell so quickly from his lips that it probably caused even him to shudder.

How weak we are, and prone to go the wrong way, as the hymn, "Come Thou Fount," so succinctly states: "Prone to wander Lord, I feel it, prone to leave the God I love. ..." Amen to that.

Peter, like Eve before him, was in the wrong place at the wrong time, which resulted in his doing the wrong thing. That is an explosive combination, and it will ultimately lead to a spiritual meltdown.

SATAN TAKES *Aim*

So in this, the first of three temptations, Satan said to Jesus, "If You are the Son of God, command this stone to become bread" (v. 3). The devil intones, "I was listening around the corner there at Your baptism to what Your Father was saying: 'You are my beloved Son; in You I am well pleased.' Seeing You are what you are, then command this stone to become bread."

Jesus shot back, "It is written, 'Man shall not live by bread alone, but by every word of God' " (v. 4). Christ was essentially saying, "I'm not here to deal with you today as

God. I'm dealing with you now as a man on man's behalf!"

"Man shall not live by bread alone. ... " In other words, Jesus was occupying ground that we, too, can occupy. He was giving us a template—an example, a model—for resisting temptation.

As we look at these three temptations, we see they were directed toward three different areas of vulnerability. The bait in the first temptation to turn a stone to bread was designed to target Jesus physically. It was the temptation to place a physical drive before a spiritual need.

"Play now, pay later."

Satan was saying, "Don't worry about the long-term repercussions of sin. Just enjoy the moment."

In other words, "Satisfy yourself. If it feels good, do it!"

"You deserve this!"

"Play now, pay later."

"What happens here stays here!"

So many will disregard, or temporarily disregard, the spiritual as they chase after the temporal pleasures this world has to offer. It is usually that cold, dead feeling sin produces that brings us to our senses and back to the God we have wandered away from. In a sense, we all are faced with this very temptation Christ faced each and every day. Each day, as His follower, you have a choice:

"Am I going to take the time to pray today, or just ignore God?"

"Am I going to look to Scripture to hear what the Lord

might say to me, or am I going to just read my newspaper instead?"

"Am I going to do the right thing, or will I merely indulge myself, given the opportunity?"

TRIVIAL *Pursuit*

Giving in to this first temptation Jesus faced is not about necessarily sinning outright. Rather, it's about allowing the trivial to outweigh the spiritual, the temporal to overshadow the eternal, and the physical to become more important than the spiritual. If a good thing takes the place of the best thing, then it can become a bad thing.

Just as surely as we hunger for food each and every day, we need to have a hunger for God's Word, which will satisfy us so that we are no longer looking to this world to fulfill our deepest needs. Job summed it up this way: "I have not departed from the commandment of His lips; I have treasured the words of His mouth more than my necessary food" (Job 23:12).

ROUND *Two*

Now Satan, frustrated with Jesus' resistance to his first temptation, comes with another that hits perhaps a bit closer to home:

> Then the devil, taking Him up on a high mountain, showed Him all the kingdoms of the world in a moment of time. And the devil said to Him, "All this

authority I will give You, and their glory; for this has been delivered to me, and I give it to whomever I wish. Therefore, if You will worship before me, all will be Yours." (Luke 4:5–7)

Note that Jesus did not refute this bold assertion. Reason being, Satan was right. Though the devil is referred to as the "Father of Lies," this time he was telling the truth. He really has control of the "kingdoms of this world"—at least for now.

When Adam sinned in the Garden, he forfeited paradise and this world to Satan, who has now become "the god of this age" (see 2 Cor. 4:4). Ephesians 2 calls him, "The prince of the power of the air, the spirit that now works in the children of disobedience" (v. 2).

THE ONLY WAY TO *Change Our World*

This is why all attempts to reform this world, culture, and society—apart from a change of heart—are ultimately futile.

Education won't do it.

Technology won't do it.

Politics won't do it.

Morality won't do it.

Religion won't do it.

Only a life changed by Jesus Christ can bring about real and lasting change. Satan is primarily the one responsible for the gross perversion, the injustice, the rabid violence, and the very rebellion against God and His laws. The devil has infiltrated politics, the media, and religion and has brought about a delusion.

But the clock is ticking for the devil. Satan knows his time is limited. He knows, being a student of Scripture, that his destruction is sure. The myth that he will one day rule hell is false, because the fact of the matter is that he will be cast into hell to be tortured, as it was created for the devil and his angels (see Matt. 25:41). But he would like to take as many with him as possible.

So for now, he is taking people captive to do his will (see 2 Tim. 2:26) and is blinding the minds of those who do not believe (see 2 Cor. 4:4).

As I said, Jesus did not refute his claim.

A SHORTCUT

But here is the point we don't want to miss about this second temptation the devil placed before Jesus. Satan was offering Jesus an opportunity to bypass the cross itself. Why would he do this? Because Jesus came to buy back that which was forfeited in the Garden.

In the Book of Revelation, which means the "the unveiling," a dramatic scene unfolds. A book, clearly of the greatest significance, is produced in heaven, but no one is able to open it:

Then I saw a strong angel proclaiming with a loud voice, "Who is worthy to open the scrolls and to loose its seals?" And no one in heaven or on the earth or under the earth was able to open the scroll, or to look at it. So I wept much, because no one was found worthy to open and read the scroll, or to look at it. (Rev. 5:1–4)

Suddenly, someone appears who can: it's Jesus.

But one of the elders said to me, "Do not weep. Behold, the Lion of the Tribe of Judah, the Root of David, has prevailed to open the scroll and to loose its seven seals." And I looked, and behold, in the midst of the throne and of the four living creatures, and in the midst of the elders, stood a Lamb as though it had been slain. … (vv. 5–6)

So, what is going on here? It is my belief that this book that only Jesus could open was, for all practical purposes, the "title deed" to the earth. This would be purchased back at a very great cost, the highest cost any one could ever pay. It would be bought back with blood—the blood of Jesus. But He would have to suffer like no other before or following in that He himself would bear all the sins of the entire human race: past, present, and future.

For Jesus, that was a fate worse than death itself.

AN OFFER YOU CAN'T *Refuse*

So Satan was offering a deal. "I know why you have come, Jesus!" the devil was saying. "You have come to purchase back that which was lost by Adam. Well, I'm going to make you an offer you can't refuse. I'll give it to you on a silver platter, if you like." But there was a catch. A big one. The devil said, "If you will give me the momentary pleasure of worshipping me, it will be yours!"

Now why would this temptation be, well, tempting? Because Satan was offering Jesus a way around the cross. And we know that although the Lord willingly bore it, He clearly dreaded it. Remember, there in Gethsemane, His "sweat became like great drops of blood" (Luke 22:44). He cried out to the Father, "If it is Your will, take this cup away from Me; nevertheless not My will, but yours, be done" (v. 42). He prayed this same prayer three times!

Satan was saying to Jesus "Just bow once. Look at all You'll gain! Surely it's worth it. The ends justify the means! Think about it, Jesus. No cross. No scourging. No Gethsemane. And most significantly, no bearing the sin of the world. Just bow before me."

RETURN *Fire*

Jesus would not, even for a moment, entertain such a wicked thought: "And Jesus answered and said to him, 'Get behind Me, Satan! For it is written, "You shall worship the Lord your God, and Him only you shall serve" ' " (Luke 4:8).

Satan said nothing about serving—just a moment's worship. But Jesus recognized that just a moment of worship can mean a lifetime of service.

It always starts with the first time. We've all heard

people say it, or perhaps we have even said it to ourselves:

"I'll only do it just this once."

"I'll know when to stop!"

"Besides, everybody's doing it."

Again, famous last words. You just reached a compromise with the hungry bear of temptation.

JUST A *Moment*

Think about how many lives have been devastated by this twisted logic. Just a moment at the altar of sexual promiscuity can lead to a lifetime of regret. That "one time" could lead to an unwanted pregnancy, even a sexually transmitted disease or HIV/AIDS.

Just a moment at the altar of adultery could lead to a ruined marriage, a destroyed reputation, and a devastated family. That's how the devil works. Give him an inch, and he'll want a mile.

Just a moment at the altar of materialism. ... When you get this one thing, this one car, this one house, this one win at the gambling table, you think that will be enough. But it never satisfies. It's never enough. It always is going to be bigger and better, new and improved.

The Bible says, "Hell and Destruction are never full; so the eyes of man are never satisfied" (Prov. 27:20).

I read an interesting article about the talented and very successful musician, Dave Matthews. Matthews is happily married, with twin daughters. He makes, in his own words, "an exorbitant living," estimated to be upwards of $20 million annually.

Yet in an interview with *Rolling Stone,* he admitted to being suicidal at times: "It comes and goes. I don't think that it will ever end. When things inside your head get kind of crazy, and you go, 'OK, let's go through the list of options. … '" He continued, "I like to drink, a lot—I think it's a healthy thing to do. But I've got a family; and I've got other things that impress me more than another drink. … I may pause, but I don't think I'll ever stop, because forever is a long time."[4]

Actor Mel Gibson once felt pretty much the same way as Matthews, but he came to a different conclusion. Gibson said, "I just got to that place where I questioned what it's all about. It was like turning into something like a circular torture-fest, just going round and round, which became an attempt by me to change the course of things, put a stop to it and take another route. …"[5] What Gibson described as his "dark night of the soul" led him to the verge of suicide. He then returned to his Christian faith. He also began to read and reread the Gospels again, specifically looking at the suffering Jesus Christ went through for us. He said that he used the sufferings of Christ to heal his own suffering. He wanted more people to know the story of Jesus, who had helped him, so Mel Gibson wrote, produced, and directed the blockbuster hit, *The Passion of the Christ.*

DON'T BOW AT THE *Altar of Compromise*

This same temptation no doubt came to Shadrach, Meshach, and Abed-Nego. They were three Jewish teenagers who found themselves in positions of power under the King of Babylon. They had been handpicked for this special assignment, and the world was their oyster.

But as time passed, the deranged ruler of Babylon, Nebuchadnezzar, had an image erected of himself and commanded all his subjects, including these three Hebrews, to bow before it. But Shadrach, Meshach, and Abed-Nego would have none of it. They knew that to bow would be idolatrous and disobedient to their God. Sure, they could have somehow justified it. They could have said, "Well, when in Babylon, do as the Babylonians do!" Or, they could have bowed and crossed their fingers behind their backs. But they knew what was right and what was wrong. And they also knew that you end up serving what you worship.

You already know how their story turned out. God delivered them from the fiery furnace of Babylon, and they were even more blessed than ever.

To Jesus, Satan offered "all the kingdoms of the world," and He refused. Others will sell out for so much less.

The Bible tells the story of a man named Esau who sold his birthright for a bowl of beans. All of his spiritual future was exchanged for temporary physical gratification.

Judas sold his soul for thirty pieces of silver.

A man named Achan forfeited his own life (as well as

the lives of his family), for a Babylonian garment.

The problem with the Father of Lies is that he may offer you something and not deliver, and yet you will still lose out. Don't bow. If you bow, you may end up worshipping. Serve God only.

THE FINAL *Temptation*

We come now to Satan's third temptation of Jesus:

> Then he brought Him to Jerusalem, set Him on the pinnacle of the temple, and said to Him, "If You are the Son of God, throw Yourself down from here. For it is written: 'He shall give His angels charge over you, to keep you,' and, 'In their hands they shall bear you up, lest you dash your foot against a stone.'"
> (Luke 4:9–11)

Notice that no one less than Satan himself is quoting Scripture here. Yet it is very important to note that as he quoted from Psalm 91, he left out something. The passage he was quoting, Psalm 91:11–12, says, "For He shall give His angels charge over you, to keep you in all your ways. In their hands they shall bear you up, lest you dash your foot against a stone."

If the devil intentionally left something out, then I want to know why, don't you? The very fact of his omission shows us immediately how important the missing words, "to keep you in all your ways," actually are to a right understanding of the text. "Your ways" is not referring to whatever path we personally choose, but in the context of the passage, it is speaking of God's ways. Once you leave that, you void out, for all practical purposes, the promises found in this powerful psalm that range from God's protection to His provision.

HAVE YOUR CAKE *and Eat It Too?*

In other words, we cannot intentionally disobey God and flagrantly violate His Word and expect His blessing and provision of angelic protection and provision. God graciously delivers some people from a situation that is a result of their own disobedience. But if they then return to the same or a similar situation, consoling themselves with the hope that God will once again get them out of this mess, then they are deceiving themselves. Don't confuse God's grace with His approval. The Bible tells us, "When the sentence for a crime is not quickly carried out, the hearts of the people are filled with schemes to do wrong" (Eccl. 8:11 NIV).

You cannot expect to be preserved if you follow sinful ways! We are to trust the Lord, not test Him.

WHAT IS THE PRIMARY WEAPON WE SHOULD USE TO *Resist Temptation?*

Let's now consider the primary weapon Jesus used to resist temptation. As I said, we are to follow His example. He stood on ground that we, too, can occupy.

Satan said, "Jump off! His angels will protect you!"

But Jesus knew the Book. His weapon was the Word of God. He responded, "It has been said, 'You shall not tempt the Lord your God'" (Luke 4:12). He was "rightly dividing the word of truth" (see 2 Timothy 2:15). Jesus didn't exercise executive privilege, but instead gave us the model of winning in spiritual warfare. And this is one of the primary weapons God has given us for winning in spiritual battle.

In Ephesians 6, the apostle Paul likens the Christian life to a spiritual battle and tells us that we are to arm ourselves for the battle. He uses a metaphor that people would have been very familiar with at the time: the armor of the Roman soldier. Among the various pieces of spiritual armor Paul mentions, such as the belt of truth, the shield of faith, and the helmet of salvation, Paul speaks of "the sword of the Spirit, which is the Word of God" (Eph. 6:17). All the other pieces of armor are defensive, with the exception of the sword, which is both a defensive and an offensive weapon. In other words, you don't attack your enemy with your helmet or shield. You attack with a sword, because it is primarily offensive in nature.

In the same way, the primary weapon for prevailing over temptation is the sword of the Spirit, the very Word of God, the Bible. If you as a believer do not have a good working knowledge of Scripture, then you will surely become a casualty in the spiritual battle.

USE IT OR *Lose It*

Sometimes people ask me to sign their Bibles, and when I do, I often write these words: "Sin will keep you from this book, and this book will keep you from sin." Satan will do everything he can to keep you from God's Word. That is just what he did with Eve. He first questioned what God had said, then distorted it, and finally added to it.

Success or failure in the Christian life depends on how much of the Bible we get into our hearts and minds on a regular basis and on how obedient we are to it. If we neglect the study of the Scripture, then our spiritual life will ultimately unravel, because everything we need to know about God is taught in the Bible. And if it can't be found in the pages of Scripture, then we don't need it.

Some people say they need more than the Bible. They claim to receive new revelations from God. But realize that if it is "new," then it is not true. If it is true, then it is not "new."

We often forget what we ought to remember and remember what we ought to forget. That is why every believer must make it a top priority to not only know the Word of God, but to also memorize it. For instance, I have memory banks to this day that are filled with obscure song lyrics and other trivial and semi-worthless information. How much better it is to have those memory banks filled with God's Word. We need to make a conscious effort to keep the Word of God at the forefront of our hearts and minds. While it's good to carry a Bible in your briefcase, pocket, or purse, the best place to carry it is in your heart.

In Deuteronomy, God commanded His people to

> "Lay up these words of mine in your heart and in your soul. … You shall teach them to your children, speaking of them when you sit in your house, when you walk by the way, when you lie down, and when you rise up. " (Deut. 10:18–19)

Once Scripture is ingrained in your memory, it will always be there to utilize. There will be times when that Scripture you memorized will pay great dividends. It will bring comfort to your heart and needed strength in a time of intense temptation. As the psalmist said, "Your word I have hidden in my heart, that I might not sin against You" (Ps. 119:11). And Psalm 37 tells us, "The law of his God is in his heart; none of his steps shall slide" (v. 31).

It is the ministry of the Holy Spirit to bring God's Word to our minds when we need it. Jesus said, "But the Helper, the Holy Spirit, whom the Father will send in My name, He will teach you all things, and bring to your remembrance all things that I said to you" (John 14:26).

Then we must use what we know. Our minds should be so saturated with God's Word that they function like spiritual computers, enabling us to remember relevant verses when we face temptation.

But the Spirit of God will not necessarily remind us of something we haven't learned. So let me ask you, what shape is your sword in? Is it polished from daily use as you study the Scripture on a regular basis? Is it sharpened on the anvil of experience as you have applied and obeyed its truth in your life? Or, is it rusty from lack of preparation or dulled by disobedience?

Victory in Jesus

4

I n closing, here is an important foundational truth to remember about temptation: We do not fight *for* victory, but *from* it. The battle has already been won by Jesus Christ at the cross.

Prior to His crucifixion, Jesus said, "Now is the judgment of this world: now the ruler of this world will be cast out" (John 12:31). Referring to this same event on Calvary, Hebrews tells us, "that through death He might destroy him who had the power of death, that is, the devil" (Heb. 2:14). The Apostle Paul reminds us that God "canceled the record that contained the charges against us. He took it and destroyed it by nailing it to Christ's cross" (Col. 2:14 NLT).

Maybe you're wondering, "If Jesus' death at Calvary was powerful and complete, then why does it appear that Satan is still on the scene, doing his dirty work?" It's because God has allowed it. That isn't a cop-out. It is simply a recognition of a temporary situation.

Remember, the enemy does nothing in the life of the Christian without the express permission of God. Jesus said to Peter, "Indeed, Satan has asked for you, that he may sift you as wheat. But I have prayed for you … " (Luke 22:31). And Jesus is praying for you too.

Every temptation that comes your way has to go through God's protective grid. Satan has to ask God's permission before he can tempt you. Such was the case with Job. Satan came to God one day, challenging the reason Job loved Him so.

> "You have always protected him and his home and his property from harm. You have made him prosperous in everything he does. Look how rich he is! But take away everything he has, and he will surely curse you to your face!"

> "Alright, you may test him," the Lord said to Satan. "Do whatever you want with everything he possesses, but don't harm him physically." So Satan left the Lord's presence. (Job 1:10–12 NLT)

Temptation is allowed, and even used, by God. But God will never give us more than we can handle.

However, if you are not a Christian, if you never have made a commitment to Jesus Christ, then you do not have this hope. You will not be able to resist temptation effectively. You are vulnerable to Satan's attacks, manipulation, and even possession.

But God loved you so much that two thousand years ago, He sent His Son to die on the cross for every sin you have ever committed. At the cross, Jesus dealt a decisive blow against Satan and his demons. The person who puts their faith in Jesus Christ no longer has to be afraid of what the devil will do, because Scripture says, "He who is in you is greater than he who is in the world" (1 John 4:4).

Is Christ living inside of you? When temptation comes knocking on my door, I like to say, "Lord, would you mind getting that?" I don't want to mess with it. It is too much for me. Therefore, I will ask the Lord to help me.

But if you are not a Christian, then you are on your own. And that is a bad place to be. Maybe you are in the throes of addiction right now. You have tried to get out. You need to say, "Lord, I am a sinner. Come into my heart and help me."

Maybe you have made a commitment Christ, but you are living in disobedience. You are trying to live in two worlds. God knows about it. Come to Him and say, "Lord, I am sick of pretending and being a liar. Help me, God. Get me out of this. I want to live for you."

If you have never come to Jesus or you need to come back to Jesus, then why don't you do that today?

Finally, let me just say that Satan isn't called the Father of Lies for no reason. When he says you will get away with something, he is lying to you. You won't get away with it. You are not the sole exception to the Scripture that says, "Do not be deceived, God is not mocked; for whatever a man sows, that he will also reap" (Gal. 6:7), or the verse that warns, "Be sure your sin will find you out" (Num. 32:23). It will come out sooner or later. Just because you got away with it yesterday and might be getting away with it today does not mean you will get away with it tomorrow.

You need to say, "Lord, I know this is wrong. I am coming to you in humility and repentance and asking you to forgive me as I turn from this sin." But if you persist in this path of disobedience, it will eventually catch up with you. You don't know how bad it could get. That is why you need to stop now.

This could be a warning from God at this very moment. He might be saying to you, "I know what you are doing. You know what you are doing. You need to stop." Maybe God is speaking to you and telling you that this is an area of your life you need to deal with.

I believe the person who is willing to say, "I have not come as far as I want to … I need to move forward, grow, learn, and stretch … I have so much ahead of me in the Lord … I want to go after it—I want to build myself up," is the kind of a person who will have a good, strong spiritual life, but not one without its problems, of course. There will be setbacks and temptations, but by and large, such a person will move forward in power.

On the other hand, for the person who is just trying to hang on, who is not learning and growing, and who toys with temptation, it will be only a matter of time until he or she will go down in defeat.

Which person are you going to be? Make that determination right now. Decide ahead of time. Will you be another victim of temptation? Or will you become a victor? Will you be conquered? Or will you be more than a conqueror? It's up to you.

If you need to make a commitment or recommitment to Jesus Christ, why not do it right now?

Here is a suggested prayer:

Lord Jesus, I know that I am a sinner. But I believe that you died on the cross for my sins and paid the price for every wrong I have ever done. I turn from that sin right now and ask you to be my Savior, my Lord, my God, and my friend. Help me to resist temptation and walk in your will from this moment forward. Thank you for hearing this prayer and that I am now forgiven. In Jesus name I pray. Amen.

If you just prayed that prayer, I would like to hear from you! You can write me at Greg Laurie, c/o Harvest Ministries, 6115 Arlington Avenue, Riverside, California, 92504.

Or, you can contact me by e-mail at Greg@harvest.org.

Also, please visit our Web site to learn more about following Christ: www.harvest.org.

Notes

1. "Little White Lies," *Bible.org*, accessed February 8, 2005: available at http://www.bible.org/illus.asp?topic_id=894.

2. "Work Excuses," *Captain Cynic*, accessed February 8, 2005: available at http://www.captaincynic.com/thread.php3/thrdid=13010-ufrmid=18.

3. Associated Press, "Crocodile Hunter Stirs Scandal with Baby Stunt," *CTV.ca*, January 3, 2004, http://www.ctv.ca/servlet/ArticleNews/story/CTVNews/1073090900773_57/?hub=Entertainment%204.

4. *Rolling Stone*, "The Devil and Dave Matthews," January 22, 2004.

5. Paul Fischer, "Gibson's Passion," *Girl.com.au*, http://www.girl.com.au/mel_gibson_passion_of_the_christ.htm (accessed February 8, 2005).

Other AllenDavid books
published by Kerygma Publishing

*The Great
Compromise*

*For Every Season:
Daily Devotions*

*Marriage
Connections*

*Are We Living
in the Last Days?*

*Strengthening
Your Marriage*

Visit:

www.kerygmapublishing.com
www.allendavidbooks.com
www.harvest.org